THE RED WE SILK

The Red We Silk

Nicole Lachat

Winner of the 2024 Michael Waters Poetry Prize

Selected by Fady Joudah

Published by the University of Southern Indiana
Evansville, Indiana

ISBN: 978-1-930508-61-3 First Edition

Printed in the USA

Library of Congress Control Number: 2025947566

This publication is made possible by the support of the Indiana Arts Commission, the National Endowment for the Arts, the University of Southern Indiana College of Liberal Arts, the USI English Department, the USI Foundation, and the USI Society for Arts & Humanities.

College of Liberal Arts

English

Foundation

We are a proud member of the Community of Literary Magazines and Presses.

Southern Indiana Review Press
Orr Center #2009
University of Southern Indiana
8600 University Boulevard
Evansville, Indiana 47712

sir.press@usi.edu
usi.edu/sir
Ron Mitchell, Rosalie Moffett & Marcus Wicker, eds.

Artwork: Benjamin Shine
Sky Flow, Quietude
Recycled HDPE mesh & steel; 15' x 8' x 3'
benjaminshine.com

Layout: Valentine Pokorney & Zach Weigand

Contents

IV

V

For my family

Let it be written: The dark days also I have praised.

–Derek Walcott

The Clerk

In this and every city, I play Charles
Aznavour when I want to swoon
in all my languages. Or hear sorrow sung

out of them. His discography on shuffle.
Each song drawing another relative
in, until suddenly we're all slow-

dancing together in the blue light
of dusk, of cornflowers, of seaside. I too want
to write each silence into a song worthy

of translation. I'm the faithful clerk of this
bloodline. I listen through the pleadings,
the arguments. I store it all, every testimony,

so we might go on together, all of us,
into the future with our histories stored
somewhere outside the body—

to remember without the pain.
I sit good and quiet to catch names.
I fashion myself into a window.

–I–

I came into poetry feeling as though, on some level, these words were not just mine but my grandparents', their parents'.

–Joy Harjo

Before My Birth

The woman that is my mother lived
as a counterfeit reflection, a specter in the hallways
of the buildings she cleaned. Inside a high-rise so tall
the night sky got caught in its mirrors, my young mother
polished the clouds and the stars.
In a borrowed name, in an ill-fitting uniform,
my mother, a steady shadow, a quick apology,
removed from the glass all evidence of life—
smudges, dust, handprints,
even her own face before dawn broke.
At the end of shift she'd coil into the back seat
of a night bus, run her hand over the sweat at her nape,
trace the stranded wisps of darkness;
and when she was sure no one was listening,
she'd untuck her name from behind
her teeth, just to affirm she was still there.

Abecedarian with Genealogy

Along la Panamericana at rush hour, the cars sit like wet
bricks. The sellers walk between cars, shouting names of products like a rescue for us
cobwebbed in Lima's traffic: *AGUA HELADA*, *CANCHITA*,
DULCES, every possible remedy for the hours ahead, for the evening heat,
every attempt at a sale. And us—trying to get back to Tía's in time
for *Magaly* to catch the latest celebrity news or
gossip. Around us, the air's perfumed with the scent of petrol and salted
hibiscus. Abuela sits beside me feigning sleep, not wanting to answer the questions
I always seem to ask: *cuéntame de tu juventud*. I am told you were married at eighteen,
just a baby. Told an uncle married you off to an older man you did not love, and you
knew nothing of the arrangement. I cannot imagine just how
lonely and loveless your face must have been beneath the veil.
Maybe we were not meant for happy endings. The women in this bloodline
never make it out unscathed. I hear the boy you loved, Alberto, stood
outside the village chapel waiting. His face rainwater under the red frangipani when you
parted. This image of him carried to Lima with you. It lived
quietly in your dreams for years. Your first husband left without
reason. Tía tells me that his ex-lover, desperate for him, *le hizo brujería*, cast
spells and made him drink of some potion the night he did not return
to you. But you didn't love him, and I wonder if you felt then, even briefly, free?
Untied from the first, another swooped in, as vultures do,
Victor, who'd give you four children and years of misery. You told me,
when I was small, he'd died, that you had no husband. But your children, my mother,
xeroxed copies of him, were daily reminders. After his infidelities,
you never let another man come to stay; but I was told that before Alberto died,
Zoilita, Tía took you to see him, that you gazed at each other—almost young again.

Chasqui

Messenger, Andean track star, I hear you calling
through the earth. You spurned distance
under your heels, carried legacy, the counted lives
of households, of armies, knotted and strung
across your chest, your waist. Prized runner,
you kept data at the touch of your fingers,
translating secrets furled in those quipus,
unknotting the beads of a people's memory.

I think I am like you, Chasqui,
always running, heavy with a burden
on my lips. Running from land to land,
never outrunning my foreignness.
Home is a thread tugging at my waist,
crumpled in my throat. I want to lay them down,
every name, rest them in the sun.
The home I left is not the same I'll return to.
Tell me, Chasqui, how many were born, how many
died since leaving. I am losing count,
and the records I left with wear thinner and thinner.
I want to make my parents proud, my mother
whom I have not touched in so long.
Did you hear your father's voice
through grasses, did water take on
your brother's face? If you do not go, Chasqui,
heavy with news from home, who will carry us
into the future?

                    I am here, now, centuries away from you,
threaded by a similar longing, a singular
pulse. I am terrified, Chasqui, of not making it
back, of arriving home with useless fingers.
If I am to speak, if my hands will make short
the long return, let them bring good news—
that there is no need for war,

there will be no fighting. The rain has come
and the crops are giving, and the sun has spun
gold enough for all of us—to say,

Look there, how it sprawls on the water,
see how it peeks through the hills.

Asking: Portrait of My Father

Still spouting fresh paint
I collect my father's eyes;
the horse in the mist is ever elusive.

On some nights he arrives
near Roussillon or Lourmarin,
in 1966.
For a kilo of peaches, he peels
off his bicycle as his brother,
strewn next to the road,
drips tomato from his chin.

Will you not show me your face?
Self-portrait as a song off my father's lips
while washing the dishes:
"Hier encore, j'avais vingt ans, je caressais le temps..."
A tune as lonely as a boy
without a brother.

Father—
When the song from the speaker turns
familiar, he is not yet nine, in a hand-me-down
robe, pouring his voice for the congregation.
When he pulls the room into his throat
    I see him.

The years before he was my father
are veil and plaster, but hold real as my desire
for heaven and his longing
for the dark nets of his brother's eyes.

Though he will not say it
from fear or doubt,
he still carries the astonishment of a child

walking under the towering heads
of sunflowers,
which is the only currency required
for the next world.

Mal Agüero

It is butterfly season: the butterflies
are busy carousing over the marigolds,
the snapdragons. I want to touch the wings,
hope one will land on my hair
and announce me beautiful. But Abuela
doesn't trust butterflies, shoos them with her arms
when they near. *Qué lindo*, I tell her as I sweep
my gaze across our back garden. Abuela
side-eyes them, watches intently as they flutter
and lift from body to body. She tells me to come away,
draws me back toward the house. *Mal agüero*, she tells me,
bringers of misfortune. Tells me not to trust
their bright orange, the metallic sheen in their movements.
She is sure of their intentions. I am just a child, she says.
She's known beautiful eyes before.

A Mother's Work

A mother weaves an aguayo she'll fit
        to her daughter like wings. Even plucks
the green feathers of the coca trees (para superar

el mal de alturas). No one asks her the cost of this,
        what it takes for her to do this sending—
how many pleadings she has brought

to the feet of night, knowing
        what she does of distance, its appetite
for daughters—but the girl

grows cloudward nonetheless,
        and the mother, weighted by what love
necessitates, bends the sky

inside herself so not to break
        the sky inside her daughter. She weaves
in what she can of wisdom

and tries to forget the story
        of the plumed boy plummeting seaward
in an orb of fire.

–II–

pájaros
locos, enamorados,
sorpresivos,
cantantes
vanidosos,
músicos migratorios
....
vagabundos,
os amo
libres,
lejos de la escopeta y de la jaula

–Pablo Neruda

The Crossing

for G. P.

I.

Entering this country was a long prayer;
we dipped across the treeline begging
the field to recognize us, to make of our bodies
a member of its grasses, its dense brush.
We could not spare bread, so we left tears
seeded along the way. We left our hope
of return. Knowing we only had one chance at this.
I clung to my son's hand, to the promise of green
growing on the other side, growing
like stacks we might hold in our hands,
like a card with my name, like permission.
Green the scent we walked through,
the field between. I made a wager
with every step that green was sweeter
than what we had left, though fear
kept me low to the ground. Every sound—
a car backfire, a siren, even a pheasant
breaking into flight—set my heart to terror.
Somewhere along the way,
a deer leapt across the horizon, jolting my body
stiff. Beneath my breath I kept asking
God, who split the sea, to keep the owner
of this farmland asleep in his bed,
to gift the patrol agent temporary blindness,
and turn us into wild geese
should any gringo
pass por aquí.

II.

In my body I carry territories:
the jungle path that runs near my tía's chakra,
the waterfalls of Huacamaillo where we bathed
and played as children, el cerro de la Merced.
I fear I will not see them again. With every step forward,
my body mourns the country that birthed me,
but this distance remains small. After all, it plagues
my tongue, it's pressed into the soft sun of my skin.
Wherever I go, white bodies seem to notice.
I will try to hide this otherness, the thick in my throat
when I say, *hel-lo.* When anxiety rises,
I will tuck behind a smile, look down to the floor,
pray no one asks to see identification.
I am asking God to see us to the other side.
I promise to stay good. I will give up
the little I have: my dancing dress,
my photo albums, my mother's house. God,
if you'll just keep this body veiled
to blue-eyed inspectors, I will make good use of my hands
and never rest idly. I will give you anything
you ask for, if you just let my son live
another kind of life.

Promised Land

In this country I'm wind-slapped

Red stain that will not dry

Elbow-deep in sand and earth

Begging stones to water

Mamá

I hear you calling me

Sleep disposes of me like a cannon

Sweat and silence land me

I gasp for air

I'm glad you're not here

Here is full of scorpions

Here the desert crossing is 500 years

And counting

Madre Mía

I wander these American avenues
looking for signs of your feet
to anchor me. Instead, only

the rumbles of cars, the chanting
of children in schoolyards,
the stiff chords of an anthem

that does not sound like you
or me. That keeps its door
narrow-narrow so the wide

brown hips of tías are left
dancing outside. But outside
the air is sweeter. It tastes

of your plantain, your lúcuma,
it goes down like un té negro
con canela y clavo de olor. Outside

doesn't bat an eye at una cholita-
gringita como yo. Sometimes,
I catch flashes of you, Ma,

in la señora de la panadería,
who passes me a quick smile
like a ticket of recognition. Her brow

all sweat and flour. And when
evening comes and I sit
quiet and alone in this apartment

that you have never seen,
when at last I press into the sofa,
all exhale, it's your wide feet

that rest on the coffee table,
it's your hands that bring el agua
de azahar to my parted lips.

Portrait of an Alien

Tía is in the kitchen with a song
on her lips for the good Lord.
Her hands are busy weeping
garlic, tomato, and onion
before they bless the pan.
Tía stores her country
in her roundness, hides its coastlines
under her shirt.

She keeps the burn
of el sol de febrero
hidden in her ají amarillo.
On the counter, fish marinates
in salt and lime. When the ceviche is set
we'll fight over who'll bring the last
of the brine to their lips. A sour
that touches the eyes, a taste
worth living for.

She's raised two sons
and the children of others
in the chapel her arms make.
Her house is telenovela,
salsas antiguas, pan con café.
On some nights, she dances through
the rooms to a music only she hears,
as if to stomp out the sorrow,
as if to soften the ground.
In her sock drawer: Saran-wrapped
packages, cat's claw, crystals of salt,
some money.

She knows it costs
to buy a glance or a smile.
She spins the same midnight

as her American neighbors,
even kneels when she prays.
But she lives between whispers
of visits at work.
She disturbs only with a hot meal,
          ointment for a body—

                    keeps her eyes down
                    when she walks.

To the Ancestors of Túpac Amaru

Beloved, this, like every thirst, does not begin with us.
Wipe your eyes. Our lineage is an ancient well
with living water. They took the river, those great white birds,

slipped in by her mouth—plucked from our trees,
plucked until gold dripped from their beaks,
until all green was touched by their landing.

Beloved, don't forget, we are a royal priesthood.
Abuelita's sweat beaded where pearls should have—
the stall and stool that curved her back bridge generations.

When the birds came, we kept our hands open,
gave seeds of maize, of papa, the good of the earth,
and they ate and they ate until our fingers bled.

What was once empire is shrunk down
to a mausoleum in the east, a boneyard, our Huayna Picchu.
But the great Inca's face still gazes from the rock.

Beloved, remember, the birds are still hungry
for every falling jewel. Even now, iron smells
of centuries. Vow never to wield it.

Under the morning mist of a pueblo joven
on the outskirts of Lima, our young mother stands
in line for a weekly ration of oats and milk.

Beloved, lift up your head. Our blood is rich
with every grief. In our clenched jaw
a fist is sprouting.

Watching American News

Ten years before my birth, my mother boarded
a plane without intention of return.

Thank you, Mamá. It's easy to say now.
Thank you, Carmen, Maria, Susana,

Yoli, all the names you walked through—
Here, you have lived a thousand lives.

Thank you for taking the flight. Thanks,
too, to the blond stranger who spoke up for you

at border security because you were entering
a language you did not yet possess.

I would tell him his kindness wove me
into possibility.

I know the grief is not mine,
but it looks like every body I love.

It is all happening live, disappearances
in the living room.

Mamá and I hold each other
as Pachamama's river runs from our eyes.

And we cannot even blink, don't dare—
we're here.

–III–

Yes, I was in that strait where
suffering changes into song.

–Adam Zagajewski

Another America

Never will I be able to know,
firsthand, what it was like to move
under the camouflage of verdure,
to resent light, to crawl between trees, bushes, wet earth
to get across an invisible line and into a country
where you have to stay on your knees.
I can't claim to know just how much of you
was lost on the journey across
or how to burn from my tongue the taste of a name
so not to forget the one you've had to give everywhere you go.
I never learned how to make myself small,
how to disappear into a thing. Breath against glass.
For two months you stayed
huddled in a house stripped raw of home,
only a few kilometers from the border,
without once stepping outside.
Tell me how to flourish as a bare wall, a doormat.
You lived so far from windows, your eyes still lick
every street clean even after all these years.
I can't know what it was like. I was born with a yelling
no one told me to hush. How many empty sinks,
white ceramic piss bowls swallowed your face,
the under-the-table, undercut pay you waited for.
I haven't had to pay the ransom for our skin.
My mothers, I was born into permission. Forgive me.

Saturday Night at the Lonely Hearts Club

Tonight, I'm somebody's
song. A name winged and heavy
lifting off the throat
of a boy I think I could bring myself to love,
if and *if* and *if*—but, I don't know more
than the harp string of his name and the shadows
he throws to music.
His voice is rife with the good sting
that I'll replay sometime in the future,
when the body feels
too singular, too slight.

Tonight, I'll pretend a future
in plural. I'll hang my "I" above the dresser,
lend my belief to the dark butterflies
inside his mouth, and lift into the brief
promise of his hands as my hands,
his waist as my waist.

Elegy for N. F.

Had there been a funeral, I would have come
mouth full of prayers, tiger lilies in my arms
to place by your side. Pomegranates too.
Only you did not die, though a country grew
between us. I wanted to reach, but frost flowered
my fingers. Windowpanes froze shut.
I lifted the phone so many nights,
but it turned to water against my ear.
We leapt from childhood together, landed
without anything to show for it. No white dress,
no dark-haired baby. I could not bear
the crisp yellow band you offered
as horizon, or the version of me
without a silver skyline, the copper glow
of Christopher Street, or the uncertainty
rumbling through my body like a night train.
Because I did not dream myself wife-sized so young
I did the only thing I knew would raze the promise
of canola fields behind me: I withheld the fire,
I swallowed whole the flame.

Supplication

At the praying wall, I try to speak
the names of those I love,
but I am a barrel overflowing
with rain. I can muster only
drowned sounds, half syllables
for each of my loved ones.
My father, high along
the mountain path,
shrinks beneath the beech
and the firs.
So many I love are dying.
I throw my salt against
the sky. Is this ache penance
for the freedom I wanted?
I close my eyes and am taken
to my mother's garden:
blue globe thistles bursting lush
with the promise of another world.
Trails of lupin lead me
like multi-colored lanterns
down toward the apple trees.
At the prayer wall, I drop my bags,
the groceries I bought along the way:
bread, lemon, leeks—
I give them.
Please, Lord, remember
my mother, though I have failed
to love her well—she who still calls
your name like an answer,
and though tired, still tilts her head
in hope to hear a reply.
Grant my parents peace. That they might
forgive their daughter
married for years to the wind.

The Year After

for Derek Walcott

A blue heron appeared before me
on what would have been your 88th birthday.
I was leaving Jambe de Bois with K. and J.,
where I'd had the accra, or was it
roti? I was nearly seeing red
as another cargo of cruise-travellers
invaded the beach at Pigeon Island,
covering every inch of sand with small dark tents.
Passing under a gliricidia in full blush,
the heron stood. There, next to the concrete staircase
planted in the hillside, the one leading nowhere
or everywhere, if above is an unseen country.
I could not help but stare at what appeared
more than a bird. In its thunderous hue,
it met my eyes, holding my gaze.
I knew then it was you come
to unfurrow my brow from the cruise's shadow,
from the sun's splintering, from my shame
of not having come to you sooner,
while there were still candles
to blow out. Having forgiven everything,
you appeared as a bird—that I might not weep
nor ask questions not yet meant to be answered.

Meditation on Touch as Love Language

It is spring again, but my body is still
working through winter's kinks.
I walk in the afternoons, take the grass
when another is coming up the pavement.
I keep my hands to myself. It's courtesy.
Still, I find myself reaching toward
the calloused skin of branches,
the green spine of leaves.
Once, my foot caught a stone and sent me
hands first into the lawn—but the dew
was such mercy that I stayed
down awhile. After trained isolation,
I confess I want to be
touched, to be held between
someone's lips like a long vowel,
to be revealed back to myself by a hand
peeling back the strap of a summer dress.

When I Said *Orange*,

what I meant was the astonishment of waking
under a clementine tree. Or the landing
of a thousand eyes over the plaza
near the duomo. Though what I meant
had nothing to do with pigeons.
Please allow me to remedy this grievance;
who was I to ascribe a hue to your eyes?

Please forgive my clumsy attempt
at touching your hand. I had not yet been
wrecked by love's rupture.
There was still so much to learn
of the ways one can be spilled.
But your hands seemed large enough
to press the body into music,
so when you said *Schubert* in the milk drip
of your Milanese, I could not help but reach—

And there, in wet sunlight
I was the color of something peeled.
So when I said *orange*, what I meant was
grant me only this:
Let me be a strip of rind on your mouth,
a burning color in your eyes.

Portrait of Returns

When the weather warms and the earth peels back
its white sheet, I return to a sun-dripped place.
The warmth of Lincoln is not the warmth of an island,
but the hunger for salt pulls my blood to another shore.

I am transported to some Friday night fete
where Gyptian's voice baptizes lovers under street lamps.
Wandering Gros Islet, I am led back to a familiar door
by the smell of bougainvillea splitting the darkness.

I am led back to hands traversing the midnight
road of my body, that draw the sea from my skin.
A man who shortens the distance of countries
in one drawing gesture.

When wandering the aisle of a grocer's,
a stack of ripening mangoes is enough to send me
back to being sun-dazed, halved by waves, licking
the residue of a salt-washed Julie mango from my palms.

And when the breeze lifts on some afternoon walk,
I am returned to The Moon, that seascape path
without the shade of acacias, where the wind mingles
with a known voice that rises and curls in my ear, an inviting tide.

Dropping My Father Off at the Airport

It was the silence afterward.
The sky not falling, the sun rising,
brandishing its color across the sky
though clouds pooled in my throat.
I was now the émigré, the lonely one.
My father had come to see me settled
and having settled me, left.
It is always easier to leave than to be left,
I'd once flaunted to those I was leaving.
As the distance between my father and I grew,
I sat in the poverty of that consolation.
For the first time "home" was a hollow sound.
I was returning to a one-room apartment
on a foreign street, where the mail comes
only to my name and only my books feel familiar.
I felt all at once the shame of teenage years
when I'd wished my parents away.
I sat within the certainty that for the first time
I did not know when I would next touch
my father's labored hands or watch a smile break
through his whitened beard as I kissed his forehead.
Grief was asking a question,
as the airport grew small behind me,
and receiving no reply.

–IV–

We tried courage, since there was no exit.

–Adam Zagajewski

The Hive

I cried so violently my father shook
as he held me. I was only eleven.
Along Mill Creek ravine my foot had grazed
a low-hanging branch housing the hive.

Before I could be gathered,
the swarm filled the air, stinging
my small frame without mercy.
Neither the shouting nor swatting

of my family would entice them to stop.
That night he and my brother waited
until the wasps had all returned to the hive
before burning it to the ground.

The pain turned my mouth to chalk, my throat
to salt. It was my first taste of weakness.
A helplessness your hands
against me, years later, revived.

I think of the currency of power
and fear. The fourteen stings eventually healed.
Is this justice? Or is it late summer,
when my brother and father,

equipped with a can of WD-40,
moved beyond the porch light's range.
Now, your face is in my mind and my eyes
betray me. But in my brother's

I see a thicket burning. So I allow you
to be small.

Clerk's Diary: Juana Doe

The gash in your lip is not a river, Juana.
There are no lilies in your bruised rib,
no matter what defense counsel says.

I write it all down, every casual exaggeration,
as you try to follow the quick switch of hand,
how language is juggled
before your one good eye.

Quick like a hand on burning stove,
like a walk in a minefield.

From the witness stand you hear your life
narrated like a movie. It is not yours,
though they play your name like a credit:

    a normal couple
    normal fights

    it only happened once

Once
quick-quick
like a screwdriver's shadow—

The Rescue

When the cry leaves me
I'll be half girl
half hunger
wolfed down by many years
of secret rendezvous
with the toilet bowl
        flushing myself from those harpies—
                voices seeding

        "Un" attractive
                "Un" worthy

When the cry leaves me
it will be after practicing
the trick
        that wave of hand
and finding no rabbit
no form enough
to render me   delicate

        "Fine" porcelain

Every time I exercise the closing act
        of disappearing
I'll transform a little more into urn

It will be all the lies fossilized
        the absence of confession to a friend   to myself
The shrine of glazed smiles
        the *I'm fine*   the fear
my teeth will fall out
        one
                at a time

It will be the acid reflux burning me into morning
        into the ER
The inability to look myself in the eyes
when brushing my teeth, and then
        the inability to look myself in the eyes

It will require
the stink   to seep   into my dreams

To cover
        every pore
        with shame

        When desperation is high
                and I'm under it—

the groan that'll leave
        the cavern
                become my body
        will sound the same
        as prayer

and that is when   God-sized hands

pull me
                out

        of the water.

Nicole,

I keep trying to write the poem
to empty out the blue
of his eyes.

You wanted to live without
the great-tailed grackle rattling
your chest, without that February.

Some nights I see red
vanishing—how feverishly he tried
to dissolve you.

Some nights I see you, again yourself,
        as if the dark chooses to gift
        a while of forgetting.

Some mornings, you lose your breakfast.
Relive the entirety of it, from beginning
to beginning—

For months you withheld
every ounce of salt
to stay afloat.

I keep trying to write the poem, Nicole,
that will spare you
his hands. The CDs on the shelf,

baladas he said he'd play for you.
Spare you the room a color
you don't remember, but struggle to leave.

Sometimes, the restaurant
where you met goes up in flames
in my head and I feel nothing,

like the tearless months
when nothing ached
because nothing was left

except cosmos vased
by the window, wilting
and reaching in the light.

You did not die, he did not
kill you, I say to the morning,
to the mirror, to the cooing dove

buried deep. It was the night sky
he tore out with his teeth.
Not me. Not me.

Clerk's Diary: Juanita Doe

What more is there to say, Juanita. Your flesh is a map of work boots. Your bones were broken small, small like the teeth in your mouth. Eleven surgeries deliver you to us, the medical chart reports. The indictment is long, *too long*, complains X. He pleads not guilty. He wasn't there. No one saw him do it. No one witnessed the blows. No one but the floors he pressed you into, no one but the walls. Here, there is a theory for everything. The courts will decide if there is enough proof—proof is the shape of your body, the steel rod in your arms. You glance over at me, lower your eyes. I am not really here. I cannot open the silence to which I am pledged. In this room I am plaster, light fixture, but I am recording. I am recording every word, your breathing, your breath. Whatever they say, Juanita, your body is testimony. I want to comfort you, to say aloud the thing you need to hear. But no matter how the defense twists the song of your bones, your body is a chorus, an encore. Each suture a singing tongue, a witness.

Crater

After years of gulping down
the bitter brine, those goblets of grief
and guilt, we gathered all the wars inside us
and wept. Next to the wide window at Remedy Café
A. and I set down every name. We lined the table
with the hands of all the men who did not love us
and did not ask—
but grinned their grins of power and took
so that our voices shrank
inside our bellies where they vanished
for years. We let out the shame of confusing
trespass with care. And in the voicing,
we did for the other what needed to be done—
we stood at the edge of those man-made craters
and witnessed into the hollow.

How to War at 3:00 A.M.

When the procession of the dead
comes knocking at your door,
do not take the candle they offer you.
Do not hold it in the hand you use
for writing or in the hand with which
you'll feed your children. Do not take
the candle. It is not a light.
It is not a cup. Its weight is
that of the long bone in your forearm.
Better yet, when the procession comes,
keep your curtains drawn,
form your mouth into the white-blue
flame, into that burning
beyond translation. Turn your hands
into cymbals.

Summer in Europe

I. *July 1995*

We cannonballed into the pool—
a pair of fireballs breaking open
the water's surface. Above us
cherries dropped casually
through the blue of summer. Some
into the pool's depths, others strewn across
the ground. We children splashed, ran, and squealed
through the garden, our lips popsicle red,
our skin reddening in the sun.

Uncle Josie, porched in a cloud of cigarettes,
watched on as we played war. Not once did we mourn
the bright cherries dropped onto hot concrete,
and we laughed
when we crushed them underfoot.

II. *February 2022 –*

All flushed with anticipation, my family
plans another European vacation.

Renewed passports come crisp and red
in priority mail. *Hell or high water*, my father says,

we can always go home. And the word falls
into our grinning like jasper in a bowl of milk

that we lap up without considering its luxury.
"Home," four letters that we've never seen

unsewn, nor pulsing beneath a missile's snout.
So, we talk pool, sun, the fat fleshy rubies we'll hang

from our ears and lips. While on a live stream,
on a red strip of land, a woman asks:

Have you seen my country—
Have you seen—

World News from America

I watch as a country fights
to remain a country. I feel helpless
in this. From my window, I lose taste
for the burnt orange of sunsets. Instead,
I imagine a boy outrunning his age
with glass bottle in hand,
the smell of petrol on his fingers
from the homemade grenade he'll use
to try and hold off his own disappearing.

And what have I done
but loafed through Sunday,
careless—bought bread, toothpaste,
ripe red fruit I ate without question—

dared to make plans.

–V–

Not that I want to be a god or a hero.
Just to change into a tree, grow for ages,
not hurt anyone.

–Czesław Miłosz

Love Poem with War Horse

Because the water is still rising
I am learning to wear the rain. I am
wearing the rubber boots, the canary raincoat.
I am practicing the art of a feather. Because you come
ready for war—swearing lightning, swearing
thunder—I come light-footed. I become
leaf. I curl at the edges
become vessel for your holding.
Because we remain intertwined
grown from the same bush
          I say is honeysuckle and you
          say is burning bush
I take your grief into my blood. I give you
the field, the pavement, I let you war.
Meanwhile, I chew on syllables, swallow whole
the letters—the hard precipice of God
that sends you hot in the blood.
I will not apologize for the faith that has been
a boat. My love, can't you see, is not in question.
But I will make room. I will become
a boat. I will widen my veins to better carry you.
You can fill this kitchen with bathwater,
you can feed us rain, and I will bring
bubbles to set you laughing, to trim back
the sky. With every downpour I am becoming canoe.
I want to talk about seeds, but no one is listening.
I want to ask about what was planted
in the field behind the Moulin, what bones the house
of Comas was built on. Understand, I want to talk
about curses. But Dad is knee-deep,
he is checking the drain, the sump pump,
sure that if he just takes it
apart, he can put the machine back together.
Mamá has laid out all her towels, she is filling pots
now, trying to collect the rain. But I have learned

to float: I keep my mouth shut, set my arms
wide open and let the water surround me.
I am tracing prayers into the dark of my lids
as your thunder passes. It has been a long season.
But the soil is ready, surely.
I am waiting on the sun. Surely,
something good and green will grow.

When They Ask What It Means to Love Thy Neighbor

Come carrying
a flashlight—extra batteries. Bring blankets
too. Come to the running water,
the crossing place, turn on your light
in the desert dark, lower your drawbridge beam.
Wave your arms like a white flag,
an invitation to dance. With jumping joy
tell them to come now—the tide is low.
Bring a smile, a translator if need be.
Show them your open palm.
Attached to the cool fire
is only a hand. The other
is reaching out.
Show them   it is safe to cross—
                             You are safe.

After the Incident

Months after believing myself
a stone, or a shard of glass, or the nothing
between stars, it returned all at once—
the pain of living: like brass striking
the bowl of my stomach or horses galloping
this field of flesh, just long enough
to convince me I was still, maybe,
soft dirt, fertile ground.
If I could hurt, perhaps
a green river
still ran through me—

How Should I Like to Flower

after Shawna Lemay

In the morning,
as a drop of milk
does in coffee.
All alone,
when my face
is still my face
and not
the stroked dazzle
of liners and creams.
As a greeting spoken
in another tongue.
In books?
In books.
As green does
between the cracks
of some edifice
witness to centuries,
privy to its secrets.
On the tips
of each
of my lover's
fingers.

Ode to Synesthesia

Call him in by the bright colors
of his name
until the whole room is dripping
golden accent, until
the saffron sound bursts
like a Roman candle in crisp
autumn air.
Linger on the *M*—the way it stains
your lips with the scent
of something nearly
delicious—call it
chocolate, that wanting,
brief sweetness.
A is always supplication—
a face burrowed in a chest, enviable.
X an axe cutting away
the questions of your body
until each breath is hal-
ved, hallowed by
the sacred sound
of ultramarine,
wet with salt
but not so
lonely.

After the Gathering

I pray my body remembers

in the days ahead

when it is too lonely

when it rains   and no one is home

to gather me

cup me from the floor   where I have pooled.

I pray my body remembers   then

your warm cheek against
mine

after we found each other

between rows of books   and ran

open-armed   to touch

histories of affection   between us.

The *I know you* *will know you* anytime.

I urge my palm to keep your pulse

hidden

that I might find it racing every once in a while

when the moon is high and your laughter

rushes from it.

I will try to carry all of it

back home with me.

When the party is over

when we disperse back

to our corners

and I am left dreaming

of your stoop

and you my patch of grass.

How holy all this has been—

this reaching for the other

and being found.

Give Me Again the Nights

Salt in our hair,
the sea reciting pages
from her antediluvian memory.

Give me again your hand in the dark,
your fingers like wind
at the base of my spine.

Give me the far light of stars,
now dead, feigning sincerity above us,
and the violet flame of your chaliced mouth.

Give them back—
the sea rushing to greet us
with the furious welcome
of a white-haired auntie
calling us by the mischief in our names.

Wonder

cannot live
wholly
in poems
it lives in the fringes
remains
tucked beneath the tongue
crouched inside the blood

To tell you
about that afternoon
at Cas-en-Bas
the sand
the colors sweeping
the sky or
the quiet miracle
of a body
at rest
in salt
would strip it
of luminance
by your very disbelief

What there was
that afternoon
is the galloping
of horses
after rain

New Year's

If you want to travel, run
around the neighborhood with an empty

suitcase in hand. At least once, full circle.
Wear yellow underwear

for the 31st lest fortune oversee your cup
as she pours. Yes, thank you. I too wish you excitement

and wealth in the New Year.
Mostly, I hope you get

through tomorrow and then the day
after. I hope you sing other than all alone

and find surprise
in the timbre of your voice.

I hope you eat well
and sleep well and go unabashed

to the doctor when you need.
I hope you see the radical beauty of a cactus,

a hedgehog, or a pasture full
of Valais Blacknose sheep grazing.

Go somewhere cerulean
without posting a thing. Be busy

loving yourself. Take a chance on
the durian.

I wish you growth, which is to say
I hope you become more tree

every day. It's easier
to become fire.

Write down your dreams as they come.
Certain births take longer.

Hope you're out there in the big
world dancing. Most importantly,

don't forget to ask.
When abuela hands you a bowl of grapes

take twelve, no more
no less. Infuse each

with a wish before you eat them.
Lord knows I've lost months to impatience.

In a year I'll let you know
just how much closer I am

to becoming a jacaranda, but
you'll know by the purple

trumpets at your feet.

Migration Song

At dusk, I read the silhouette of Canada Geese across the sky.
Their sharp formation a cutting verse, an arrow, a victory.
The shape of fingers making their way back to prayer.
The geese are going home again, warmth is returning
to the soil, the air. They ride its current northward.
The skein carries distance in their bellies, their blood
recites the coordinates of balsam poplars and saskatoons.
Having learned the cost of departure, I too crave return.
Faithful, I trace their letters from America. I know
the pulsing of the blood that draws them homeward,
how home becomes remembrance, vowels uttered
in sleep. I covet their flight. How gently they expose
the farce of borders. Beneath their wings, checkpoints vanish
like sullen shadows. Soon, they'll land in Hawrelak Park.
I wish I were home to greet them, to witness their arrival;
how they crease the sky's reflection in the folds of their wings
and scatter the remains of evening light across the water.

Homecoming

In late spring, when the apple trees speak bud and flower,
I think of my father: his torso vanishing into the high branches,
those in the front yard and the back garden.
Years ago, he grafted onto what were single trees
two more legacies. So now each gives Macintosh, Goodall,
and Norland. The grafted branches grew so close and well,
we cannot tell which came first. And each year the branches grow taller
on those trees that look so much like us, our mixed family.

All summer, his hands speak of the swollen fruit
he gathers into tall plastic buckets, then heaves into the house
for peeling, cutting, and freezing so there might be pies
all winter. Nothing is ever cast to waste. The bruised apples,
too, collected from the ground, the ones thinned by late frost
or torn by the mouths of wasps, are boiled
down into syrup for sauce and jam.
On some early August mornings, he vanishes into the cool
of the garage where he presses apple after apple
into pulp and juice until my mother calls him back
for coffee and crumble.

Now, when the white-pink blossoms round the air
like tender cheeks a daughter might lean up to kiss,
I am next to my father, ready for the tangy sweet fragrance
that lives all summer in that house—
trapped beneath his fingernails, tucked behind his ears.

Recurring Dream

I am trying to make it back to the ancestral field,
back to the chakra where the tías are waiting
having wrapped and steamed the juanes,
boiled and peeled the aguaje for its custard
pulp. They are waiting for me, I know this
with the knowing reserved for dreams, in that open-
aired kitchen, that kingdom of their own
where plantains hang like chandeliers.
But I have wandered far, lured by birdsongs
flitting off branches and the torch tail
of the oropendola blazing
through the ceiba trees.

Notes

The epigraph for this collection is from Derek Walcott's poem "26" from *The Bounty.*

The section I epigraph is from Joy Harjo's "Beyond Language" interview conducted by Layli Long Soldier for the Poetry Foundation.

"Chasqui": Quipus were a device for recording information used by the Incan Empire. Made of thread, each knot made held a different meaning/message. Chasquis were some of the few who were able to translate the quipus.

"Asking: Portrait of My Father": The song referenced is "Hier Encore" by Charles Aznavour.

The section II epigraph is from Pablo Neruda's poem "Oda a mirar pajáros."

"Promised Land": "Begging stones to water" is a reference to Exodus 17:6.

The section III epigraph is from Adam Zagajewski's poem "Franz Schubert: A Press Conference" from *Tremor.*

The section IV epigraph is from Adam Zagajewski's poem "Life is Not a Dream" from *Eternal Enemies.*

The section V epigraph is from Czesław Miłosz's acceptance speech for the 1980 Nobel Prize in Literature.

"How Should I Like to Flower": The title is inspired by the opening line of Shawna Lemay's poem "Cocktail Party" in the collection *Asking.*

Acknowledgments

Many thanks to the editors of the publications in which the following poems have previously appeared, sometimes in different forms:

Birdfeast Magazine: "Before My Birth"
Fourteen Hills: The SFSU Review: "Promised Land"
Nebraska Writers Collective: "Ode to Synesthesia"
One by Jacar Press: "Nicole,"
Palimpsest Magazine: "Another America"
Poets.org: "The Crossing"
Southern Indiana Review: "The Clerk" and "Elegy for N. F."
Tinderbox Poetry Journal: "New Year's"

Many, many thanks to the team at SIR who have supported this manuscript and have helped bring it to life. With a special thanks to Ron Mitchell for walking me through this process. And to Fady Joudah who selected *The Red We Silk* for the Michael Waters Poetry Prize.

My deepest gratitude to Derek Walcott, my first mentor—I carry you always, Professor.

To the wonderful teachers of the craft that have walked with me at various stages, including Bert Almon, Yusef Komunyakaa, Shawna Lemay, Catherine Barnett, and Canisia Lubrin. I am so grateful for your voices.

And to the incomparable Kwame Dawes—where would I be without you, boss? Thank you for your continued guidance and faith, and for occasionally talking me down the ledge of my unreason.

I am thankful to the English Department at the University of Nebraska-Lincoln and to the professors who have supported this work in various ways, particularly my exceptional committee members: Hope Wabuke, Stacey Waite, and Luis Othoniel Rosa.

Thank you to the Banff Centre for Arts and Creativity, the CAS Student Writing Retreat at Cedar Point Biological Station, and the Nebraska Arts Council for providing spaces and provisions that make the writing possible.

I am grateful to the friends with whom I share in the joys and sorrows of this writing life, including Alycia Pirmohamed, Adi Onita, Kendel Hippolyte, Jane King, Tryphena Yeboah, Jessica Poli, and also Tara and Chaun Ballard and Jihyun Yun, who patiently read version after version of these pages.

And to Zainab Omaki, without whom I would have become an island.

To Elliott, Ieva, Dennis, Arlene, Ken, Marie, Jeannie, Jeff, Heather, Mayri, and all the saints who have helped carry my mat, thank you. And to Yolaine, who has kept me—words cannot express. Thank you for sharing your luminous spirit.

Kelta, Kasia, Chan, Rachel, Cristina, thank you for our histories of love, for cheering me through the big and the small stuff.

Amadis, Nancy, los bebes, Gladys, abuelita Zoila, y toda mi familia—los quiero.

Mami, Papou, and Bawbs—words will fail here. I am indebted to your unrelenting love. Thank you for shouldering me every day of my life. There is no I without you. I will never be able to fully repay. Thank you for making every sacrifice.

Y por todos aquellos que han cruzado con miedo y a pesar de el.

Ante todo, gracias, Señor. Thank you, Lord.